CW01309724

You Were Meant To Be!

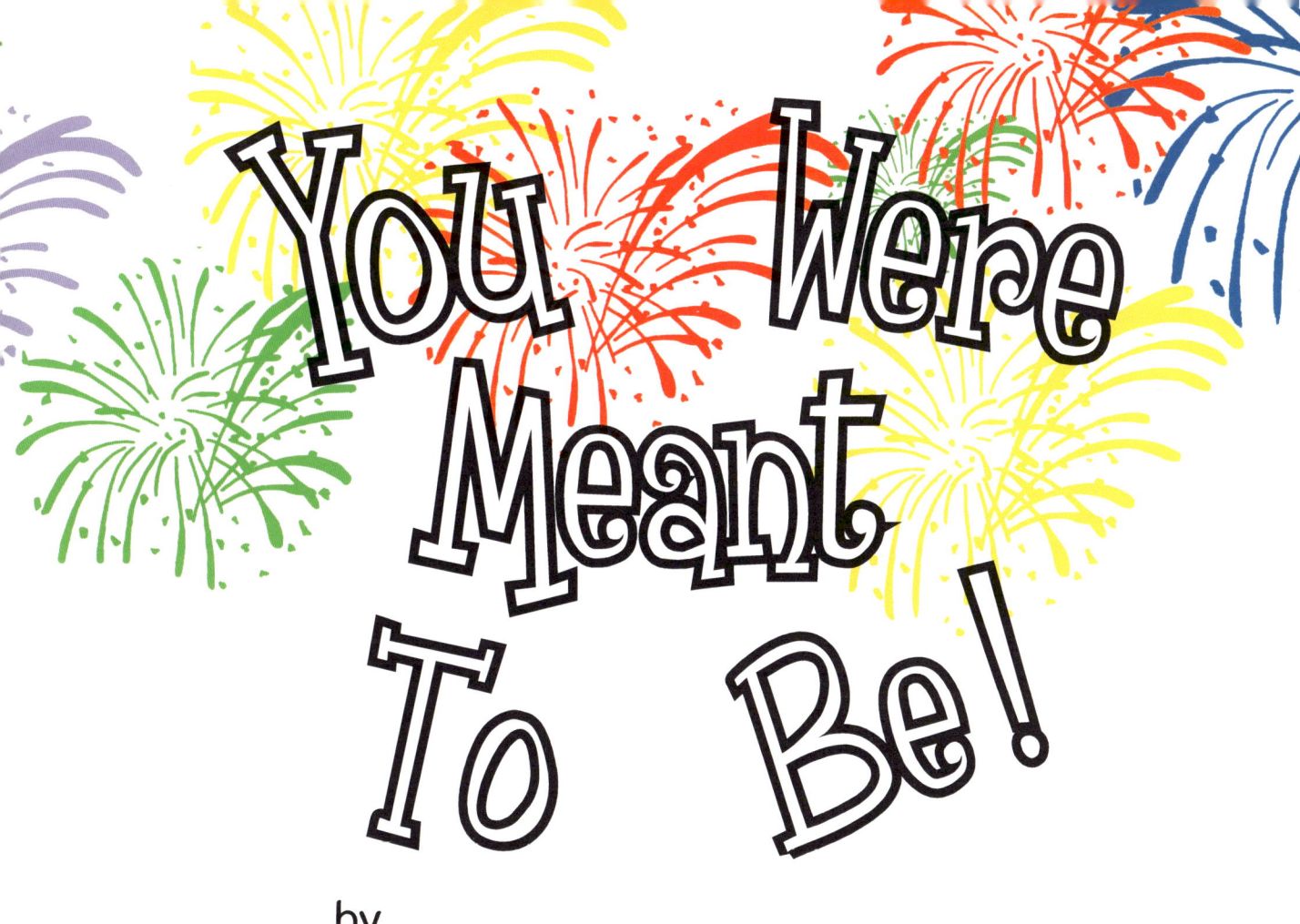

by
Sherry Keen

illustrated by
Rosemarie Gillen

Copyright © 2013 Sharon Keen

Big Tent Books

115 Bluebill Drive
Savannah, GA 31419
United States

All rights reserved. No part of this book may be reproduced or transmitted in any form or by any means, electronic or mechanical, including photocopying, recording or by an information storage and retrieval system – except by a reviewer who may quote brief passages in a review to be printed in a magazine, newspaper or on the Web – without permission in writing from the author.

This book was published with the assistance of the helpful folks at DragonPencil.com

This book is dedicated
to my two boys who have brought me
love and joy unparalleled by all else

You were meant to be

You were meant for me

You are special and
UNIQUE,
not like any one else in the whole world.

You are one of a kind,

like a *shimmering* snowflake,

or a BEAUTIFUL butterfly,

or a *twinkling* star.

But

HOW

did you get here?

It takes a piece from a woman and a piece from a man to make a baby.

They each have something that fits **TOGETHER** like a puzzle.

A woman's puzzle piece is called an egg

and a man's puzzle piece is called sperm.

When these two pieces come together they can

GROW

into a baby.

Sometimes, for many reasons, a man or a woman cannot have a baby.

Maybe a puzzle piece is

missing

or does not work.

Your family was missing a piece of the puzzle, but we wanted you

SO MUCH

that we found a way to replace it.

But where did we get the missing piece?

There are kind and generous people who want to *help* others make a family.

They donate their egg or sperm to people who **NEED** them.

Sometimes we know our donors, or sometimes the donors want to stay **a n o n y m o u s.**

Either way, we are very grateful that they helped us get YOU

The most important thing for you to know is how *special* you are, how much you are

LOVED,

and that...

you   were

meant to be!

CPSIA information can be obtained at www.ICGtesting.com
Printed in the USA
BVIW12n0936130818
524339BV00008B/11